How to Run a
Meeting

Mary A. De Vries

Based on
The New Robert's Rules of Order

REGISTERED TRADEMARK—MARCA REGISTRADA

- How many "tellers" are needed for voting by ballot?
- Can a motion to adjourn be reconsidered?
- Does a Call for Orders of the Day need to be seconded?
- Does a motion to limit or close debate need a majority or a two-thirds vote to pass?
- Can the chair vote if the voting is done by ballot?
- Does the treasurer need to be bonded?
- Can the chair close debate if a motion has been made and seconded to close the discussion but someone still wishes to speak on the issue?

YOU WILL FIND THE CORRECT ANSWERS IN SECONDS WITH

The portable, on-the-spot voice of authority for officers and attendees

MARY A. DE VRIES is the author of more than thirty-five books. Having arranged and conducted hundreds of meetings of all sizes, she is also the editor of ten books of conference proceedings. An expert in parliamentary procedure, her writings include *The New Robert's Rules of Order,* as well as *The New American Dictionary of Abbreviations, The New American Handbook of Letter Writing and Other Forms of Correspondence,* and *The Complete Office Handbook,* all available from Signet paperbacks. She lives in Sedona, Arizona.

HOW WOULD YOU RULE?

- How many "tellers" are needed for voting by ballot?
- Can a motion to adjourn be reconsidered?
- Does a Call for Orders of the Day need to be seconded?
- Does a motion to limit or close debate need a majority or a two-thirds vote to pass?
- Can the chair vote if the voting is done by ballot?
- Does the treasurer need to be bonded?
- Can the chair close debate if a motion has been made and seconded to close the discussion but someone still wishes to speak on the issue?

YOU WILL FIND THE CORRECT ANSWERS IN SECONDS WITH

How to Run a
Meeting

The portable, on-the-spot voice of authority for officers and attendees

---

MARY A. DE VRIES is the author of more than thirty-five books. Having arranged and conducted hundreds of meetings of all sizes, she is also the editor of ten books of conference proceedings. An expert in parliamentary procedure, her writings include *The New Robert's Rules of Order,* as well as *The New American Dictionary of Abbreviations, The New American Handbook of Letter Writing and Other Forms of Correspondence,* and *The Complete Office Handbook,* all available from Signet paperbacks. She lives in Sedona, Arizona.

How to Run a
Meeting

Mary A. De Vries

Based on
The New Robert's Rules of Order

A PLUME BOOK

PLUME
Published by the Penguin Group
Penguin Books USA Inc., 375 Hudson Street,
New York, New York 10014, U.S.A.
Penguin Books Ltd, 27 Wrights Lane,
London W8 5TZ, England
Penguin Books Australia Ltd, Ringwood,
Victoria, Australia
Penguin Books Canada Ltd, 10 Alcorn Avenue,
Toronto, Ontario, Canada M4V 3B2
Penguin Books (N.Z.) Ltd, 182-190 Wairau Road,
Auckland 10, New Zealand

Penguin Books Ltd, Registered Offices:
Harmondsworth, Middlesex, England

First published by Plume, an imprint of Dutton Signet, a division of Penguin Books USA Inc.

First Printing, April, 1994
10 9 8 7 6 5 4 3 2 1

LIBRARY OF CONGRESS CATALOGING IN PUBLICATION DATA: 93-85133

Printed in the United States of America
Set in New Baskerville
Designed by Leonard Telesca

Contents

Committee Meetings 31
Rules That Apply to Committees 31
When a Committee Concludes Its Work 31

Committees of a Deliberative Assembly 32
Types of Committees 32
Matters Referred to a Committee 33
Executive Session 33
Committee of the Whole 34

Committee Reports 35
Reporting to an Assembly 35
Receiving a Report 36
Adopting a Report 36

4. Introduction of Business 38

The Agenda 38
Order of Business 38
Soliciting Topics 38

Introduction of Business 39
How to Introduce Business at a Meeting 39
Obtaining the Floor 39
How to Make a Motion 40
The Chair's Duties 40
Modifying a Motion 42
Dividing a Motion 42

Rules of Debate 43
How to Open Debate 43
Guidelines for the Chair 43

Voting Procedure 44
How to Put a Motion to a Vote 44

5. Motions 46

Preface

How to Run a Meeting is a simplified, quick-reference guide to proper meeting procedure based on General H. M. Robert's famous *Robert's Rules of Order* (1893) and the expanded modern version of this classic published by the New American Library in 1989: *The New Robert's Rules of Order.*

This condensed version of the rules of parliamentary procedure was prepared for officers and members of ordinary organizations who want to have a brief pocket reference to consult at meetings without having to wade through a detailed, often-complicated, full-version text. This is not to suggest that a complete text on parliamentary law and practice is not necessary. It is. But most of the time, the points of meeting procedure that concern officers and meeting attendees can be understood and decided without taking time to peruse and study a detailed explanation. A simplified, condensed version of the basic rules and practices is indispensable for rapid reference in the midst of meeting proceedings.

How to Run a Meeting includes most of the essential topics provided in the original *Robert's Rules of Order.*

- Chapter 1 outlines the origins of parliamentary law and explains how it developed in the United States.
- Chapter 2 looks at different kinds of meetings and de-

scribes procedures in meetings of both organized and un-organized groups.

- Chapter 3 describes the duties of the officers, including instructions on preparing the meeting minutes, and explains the function of committees.
- Chapter 4 tells you how to introduce business at a meeting, including how to handle motions and put them to a vote.
- Chapter 5 summarizes the principal rules that apply to the important motions described in *Robert's Rules of Order.* *(Note:* Throughout the text these motions are capitalized to distinguish them from other motions that might be made in a meeting.)

Several aids to fast reference are used throughout these chapters, such as sample dialogue to illustrate how to word motions and other statements, as well as a margin index to help you locate topics quickly during a meeting. A glossary at the end of the book will help you recognize the special terminology used in parliamentary practice.

Although a condensed version cannot take the place of a detailed rules-of-order text, this book has other important advantages.

- Because of its more manageable size and simplified presentation, you can use it more easily than a large book for at-a-glance information.
- Since you can locate key rules and procedures quickly, you can make correct on-the-spot decisions without delaying the proceedings.
- Often a full text has more extensive detail than you need and causes the subject to be unnecessarily complex and difficult; a condensed version pares everything down to the briefest, simplest facts, making it much easier to understand.

Using a condensed version alone or as a supplement to a full text should enable you to conduct or attend a meeting with complete confidence that you'll do and say the right things.

1 Parliamentary Law

Meaning of Parliamentary Law

It's easier to learn how to do something if you understand the terminology that others are using. Many people are nervous about meeting conduct because the terminology sounds so formal and complicated. Some of it is complex, but you don't need a law degree to understand basic terms such as *parliamentary law* and *parliamentary procedure*.

❑ Parliamentary Law

Parliamentary law refers to the rules, precedents, and customary practices that apply to meeting conduct in deliberative assemblies and other organizations. The adjective *parliamentary* comes from the word *parliament,* a governing body that was officially established in England around the thirteenth century. The term describes an assembly of people gathered together to discuss common interests and decide on a course of action. That description of a parliament can be applied to any deliberative assembly.

❑ Parliamentary Procedure

Parliamentary procedure is a related term that is often used interchangeably with *parliamentary law.* Any distinction is too slight for most people to worry about, but *parliamentary procedure* is sometimes used primarily in reference to the actual steps you would take in following parliamentary law or implementing any other rules of meeting conduct, such as what you would say or do and when you would say or do it. *Parliamentary law,* on the other hand, is sometimes used primarily in reference to the principles or rules themselves, as opposed to their implementation.

The Birth of Parliamentary Law

❑ Parliamentary Practice in Primitive Societies

You could make a case that primitive societies used a form of parliamentary practice if you think of parliamentary law in very general terms as follows: any set of rules that is imposed by someone in control, or by some group in control, on a body of people gathered to discuss something and decide on a plan of action. In that broad and general sense, cave people were possibly the first to use the rudiments of contemporary parliamentary law.

❑ Parliamentary Practice in England

Historians point to stirrings of parliamentary practice in Anglo-Saxon England as early as the fifth century. A more specific example of early parliamentary practice is the operation of Norman councils. These councils, created by Norman kings after the Norman Conquest in the eleventh century, could be considered the forerunners of the first English parliaments, where the seeds of formal parliamentary law initially sprouted.

By the late sixteenth century in England, the House of Commons had developed a written record, called the *Journal of the House of Commons,* that outlined English parliamentary procedure. In time, these early rules and practices were further refined, and other organizations, including the assemblies in English colonies, adopted the resulting parliamentary practices. By the seventeenth century, the basis of parliamentary law had spanned the Atlantic to reach the shores of the North American continent.

Parliamentary Law in The United States

❑ Parliamentary Practice in the Colonies

Parliamentary law in the United States started in the colony of Virginia, formed in 1607, and spread throughout the other colonies. These colonies, however, were each established under different conditions, defined by various written documents, such as different company charters. They therefore had different needs, and the English-based rules and practices were applied differently as circumstances warranted. Already, you could see the first deviations from English parliamentary law occurring in colonial America.

❑ Early Postcolonial Parliamentary Law

The events of history changed the character of American settlement forever, and the development of state constitutions and other documents, following the Declaration of Independence in 1776, changed the nature of formal codification and associated parliamentary rules and practices in the United States. Nevertheless, even though parliamentary law in a new America was being tailored to new American requirements, it was firmly entrenched. U.S. parliamentary law and procedure represented the authority on which postcolonial governmental meeting conduct relied.

❑ Jefferson's Manual of Parliamentary Practice

The U.S. parliamentary system is still evolving, as various refinements continue to be made from time to time. But one of the most notable advances occurred earlier in American history, when Thomas Jefferson's *Manual of Parliamentary Practice* was published in 1801. Although prepared for use in American institutions, Jefferson's book borrowed from English documents, such as the *Precedents of Proceedings in the House of Commons,* prepared by John Hatsell, who was clerk of the House of Commons from 1768 to 1820. Throughout the United States, national, state, and local governmental and legislative bodies, including the U.S. Senate and House of Representatives, adopted the rules that Jefferson compiled.

❑ Cushing's Manual of Parliamentary Practice

It wasn't long, though, before ordinary nongovernmental and nonlegislative groups wanted to have a set of rules more suited to their own needs. In 1845 the first work to move in that direction was published: *Manual of Parliamentary Practice: Rules of Proceeding and Debate in Deliberative Assemblies,* by Luther S. Cushing. But "Cushing's Manual," as it was popularly called, still left many needs unfulfilled in ordinary groups.

❑ Robert's Parliamentary Rules

The demand for something more applicable to ordinary organizations caught the attention of an army officer, Henry Martyn Robert, when he had to conduct a meeting in 1863 and discovered firsthand what he *didn't* know about parliamentary law and procedure in meetings. A little more than a decade later, Robert began writing what would become the best-known guide to parliamentary law and procedure in the United States: *Robert's Rules of Order.*

Robert's Rules of Order

❑ A Work for Ordinary Organizations

Robert believed that America needed a parliamentary guide "based . . . upon the rules and practice of Congress, and adapted . . . to the use of ordinary societies," and his work reflected that belief. The first edition of *Robert's Rules of Order* was published in early 1876, and the second edition was published about five months later. A third edition followed in 1893. Various revised versions have appeared since then, and most organizations today use parliamentary systems that are based in full or in part on the original work of General Robert.

Robert believed that the rules of the U.S. House of Representatives were better suited to ordinary meetings than were those of the Senate. The rules in his original book and subsequent editions, therefore, are very similar to the House rules, with occasional minor changes recommended for ordinary groups.

❑ Content of Robert's Rules of Order

The complete text of the original *Robert's Rules of Order* is presented in three main parts:

Part I. Rules of Order: Introduction to Business, General Classification of Motions, Motions and Their Order of Precedence, Committees and Informal Action, Debate and Decorum, Vote, The Officers and the Minutes, Miscellaneous

Part II. Organization and Conduct of Business (a simplified parliamentary primer based on Part I): Organization and Meetings, Officers and Committees, Introduction of Business, Motions, Miscellaneous

Part III. Miscellaneous: Legal Rights

The language in the earlier editions of *Robert's Rules of Order* is vintage English and is often cumbersome to read and difficult to understand. People who are uncomfortable with archaic prose should use a more recent version of the classic 1876 and 1893 editions that has been written in contemporary English.

2 Organized Meetings

The Nature and Purpose of Meetings

❑ Face-to-Face and Electronic Meetings

If two or more people have a common interest and need to discuss something or decide on some action to take, they usually come together to hold a face-to-face meeting or, increasingly today, establish an electronic link to hold a teleconference. If a teleconference is voice only (telephone), it is called an *audioconference*. If it includes sound and pictures (television), it is called a *videoconference*.

Special Meeting Terms. Informally, the word *meeting* is used to mean any type of gathering for the purpose of discussing something or making decisions about something. In formal meeting conduct, however, a distinction must be made between a *meeting* and a *session* and between a meeting *adjournment* and a *recess*. (For additional terms, refer to the glossary.)

- *Meeting:* A single body, or assembly, of people in one location in which the attendees do not separate except for a short recess.
- *Session:* A series of meetings during which the business being transacted or the program being presented is continued from one meeting to another.
- *Adjourned meeting:* A meeting that is a continuation of a regular or special meeting. It is held at a later time but before the next regular session.
- *Adjournment:* The termination of a meeting. (If the mem-

bers won't meet again, unless a special session is called, until the next time prescribed in the bylaws, the adjournment is *sine die,* or without day.)

- *Recess:* A less formal break than an adjournment, after which business continues where it left off without formally opening the proceedings as one would do after an adjournment.

❏ Rules for Meeting Conduct

Reason for Rules of Order. Whether business is transacted electronically or in person, an organized meeting of any size must be conducted according to the rules of order that the group or organization has adopted. Without rules of order, a gathering could easily deteriorate into noisy chaos, with no established authority to draw on. Also, members who oppose certain decisions might contest their legality on the grounds that the group had no official rules to govern the motions and to validate majority (or other) decisions and bind the group to abide by them.

Need to Control Large Groups. The size of a meeting is an important consideration in the application of rules of order. The larger the meeting, the more precise the planning, organization, and conduct must be. To manage a large crowd, it is especially important that the organization have a parliamentary authority to guide its conduct. This will insure that everyone is treated equally and that no one can legitimately question the chair's fairness in matters of debate and decision making. Even very small organizations, however, must use proper rules of order to insure fairness of and give validity to their actions.

Adoption of a Parliamentary Authority. Since conducting business without official parliamentary rules is so risky for organizations of any size, one of the first things that a group or an organization should do is vote to adopt a parliamentary authority as its official, binding rules of order and procedure. For an example of a motion to accomplish this, see the section "Constitution, Bylaws, and Other Rules," page 17.

Reason for Rules

Large Groups

Parliamentary Authority

❑ Classification of Meetings

Broad and Narrow Classifications. You can classify meetings almost any way you choose. An example of a broad classification is by type of scheduling, such as regular (e.g., weekly or monthly), annual, and special. The constitution and bylaws of an organization specify the requirements concerning regular, annual, and special meetings—number to be held, notification requirements, and so on. *(Note:* In a special meeting, only the designated purpose for the meeting, as stated in the notice, may be discussed.)

An example of a more precise classification of meetings is by type of attendee: directors, stockholders, departmental heads, governors, Republicans or Democrats, parents, teachers, students, city council members, and so on. This type of descriptive classification can be expanded indefinitely to include the meetings of every imaginable group in existence.

Occasional Mass Meetings

Some of you may be concerned with the proper conduct of an occasional mass meeting of an unorganized group. Those sponsoring this type of meeting, such as one or more concerned residents of a large community housing development, might want to encourage the invited audience to take some action to enhance the community's status or to prevent others from doing something that will harm them.

❑ Meeting Notice

The person or group calling the meeting should issue a call, or announcement, by some appropriate method or combination of methods that will best reach the desired audience: newspapers, radio or television, posters, mailings, telephone, or electronic communication (E-mail, fax, telex, and so on).

Content of the Notice. The notice must state the date, time, place, purpose, and intended audience. Most meeting notices

Meeting Classification   Occasional Mass Meetings   Meeting Notice

are very brief, stating only the essential facts. But sometimes, in the case of an occasional mass meeting, the attendees are not familiar with the matter to be discussed. The notice, therefore, may be prepared as a one-page letter or bulletin that provides detailed background information intended to motivate recipients to attend.

❑ Selecting a Chair and a Secretary

The sponsors should decide in advance who will open or chair the meeting, who will take the minutes and what type of backup recording will be used, and what rules of order will govern the proceedings.

Electing a Chair. The person selected to initiate proceedings might begin by standing and stating:

Will the meeting please come to order? My name is _____.

An alternative procedure would be for the sponsors to arrange for someone to step forward and state:

The meeting will please come to order. I move that _____ *act as chair of this meeting.*

Another person should reply:

I second the motion.

The first person would put the motion to a vote:

It has been moved and seconded that _____ *act as chair of this meeting. Those in favor say aye. Those opposed, no.*

If a majority vote in favor:

The motion is carried. _____ *will take the chair.*

Electing Chair

In the unlikely event that a majority would *not* confirm the proposed chair, the person opening the meeting must ask for other nominations and for a second to each nomination. When nominations appear to have ended, the person presiding should ask if there are any further nominations and then, if there are none, declare the nominations closed (without formal motion). But if nominations continue to the point of excess, without apparent end, someone should make a motion to close the nominations. After a second is made, the person who opened the meeting should ask for a vote on the motion that nominations cease.

Each name on the list of nominees must then be put to a vote. This is often done by asking the audience to say aye or no or by asking for applause after each name. Upon conclusion, the person who opened proceedings should announce the winner and turn the meeting over to the new chair. (See the section "Assembly of Delegates," page 11, for instructions on using a nominating committee instead of asking for nominations from the floor.)

Electing a Secretary. The newly elected chair would continue the meeting by asking for someone to nominate a secretary, following the same voting procedure used to elect a chair. Here, too, each nomination must be seconded, and after nominations have closed, each name must be voted on and the winner announced. The person elected secretary must immediately begin taking minutes of the meeting proceedings. (See Chapter 3 for more about the positions of chair and secretary.)

❑ Statement of Purpose

After the secretary is elected, the chair can focus on the purpose of the meeting.

You have been invited here tonight to _____.

If a particular matter is to be voted on as well as discussed, the chair should ask for a motion, ask for a second, and ask if there is any discussion. (In a large meeting, where names and faces are unfamiliar, the chair should ask people to stand and state their names when making and seconding motions.) When no further discussion is desired, the chair can put the motion to a vote:

It has been moved by _____ and seconded by _____ that _____. Those in favor say aye. Those opposed, no. The motion has carried [or has failed].

Chapters 4 and 5 provide further information on motions and the proper way to introduce them.

Assembly of Delegates

Some large meetings consist of specially selected attendees, such as members of a political party at a political function. A different procedure to initiate proceedings is required in a convention and an assembly of delegates.

❑ Credentials Committee

Appointment of a Credentials Committee. When members or delegates are elected or appointed to attend a meeting, rather than merely invited, before forming a permanent organization a committee on credentials is needed to verify who is entitled to vote. First, a temporary organization can be formed by asking someone to nominate a chair pro tem, asking someone to second the motion, and putting the motion to a vote. If the nominee is elected (if not, see the procedure in the section "Occasional Mass Meetings," page 8), he or she might state:

We need to begin by appointing a committee on credentials. May I have a motion to that effect?

Someone should respond by stating:

Assembly of Delegates

Credentials Committee

I move that a credentials committee of three be appointed by the chair pro tem.

The committee on credentials should follow the instructions given in Chapter 3 on drafting resolutions and preparing a committee report.

❑ Election of Permanent Officers

Appointing a Nominating Committee. The chair pro tem can now move on to the election of permanent officers of the assembly. To create a nominating committee, someone might state:

I move that the chair pro tem appoint a nominating committee of three to nominate permanent officers of this assembly.

If the motion carries, the nominating committee will meet to prepare a report that, after presentation to the assembly, will be put to a vote. Following the presentation, someone might state:

I move that the report of the nominating committee be accepted and that the officers the committee has nominated be declared the officers of this assembly.

See Chapter 3 for information on adopting a committee report.

Voting. If there is more than one nominee for any office, it will be necessary to introduce balloting or any other approved method of voting to select the officers. Common voting methods are acclamation (aye or no), show of hands, standing vote, secret ballot, and roll call. If secret ballots have been distributed, collected, and counted, or if a precise count has occurred by some other method, the chair pro tem might state the following for each office:

Electing Officers

Nominating Committee

Voting

The number of votes cast for the office of _____ is _____. The number necessary for election is _____. Ms. _____ received _____; Mr. _____ received _____. Mr. _____, having received the required number, is elected _____ of the assembly.

Otherwise, a more general statement could be provided, such as:

Ms. _____ has received a majority and is elected _____ of this assembly.

Permanent Organization: First Meeting

Unlike an occasional meeting of an unorganized group, a meeting to form a permanent organization is usually attended by people who want to participate in the regular activities of the proposed organization.

❑ Meeting Announcement

The announcement of a first meeting to form a new organization can be made the same way that a call is issued for a mass meeting, as described in the section "Occasional Mass Meetings," page 8. The date, time, place, purpose of the meeting, and invited audience must be provided in the announcement.

❑ Opening the Meeting

Electing a Chair and a Secretary. Prior arrangements should be made by the organizers of the meeting—the people who want to form the new organization—for someone to step forward and state:

The meeting will come to order. I move that _____ act as chair of this meeting.

First Meeting

Meeting Announcement

Electing Chair, Secretary

If the motion is seconded and passes, the new chair can move on to the election of a secretary. (If there is more than one nomination for the position of chair or secretary, follow the procedure described in the section "Occasional Mass Meetings," page 8.)

❑ Statement of Purpose

The elected chair will state, or will ask someone else to state, the reason for calling the meeting:

We've asked you to meet here today to discuss the formation of a new organization to _____.

Resolution to Form Organization. After concluding the introduction or discussion about the proposed organization, the chair pro tem might read a resolution previously prepared by the organizers.

RESOLVED, That it is the opinion of this meeting that an association for _____ should be formed.

Or, more simply:

RESOLVED, That this meeting has been called to form an association for _____.

After someone seconds the resolution and discussion is opened to the attendees, a vote should be taken. If it carries, the movement to form a new organization can proceed to the next step, appointing a constitution and bylaws committee.

❑ Appointment of Constitution and Bylaws Committee

To form a constitution and bylaws committee, someone might propose the following:

I move that the chair appoint a committee of five to draft a constitution and a bylaws and that it report at an adjourned meeting.

After receiving a second to the motion and a vote on having the chair appoint a constitution and bylaws committee, the chair should ask if there is any other matter to consider before adjourning.

❑ Adjournment

If there is no other business, the chair might ask for a motion to Adjourn to meet at a certain time and place. After a second to the motion and an affirmative vote, the chair could conclude the meeting by restating the designated time and place:

This meeting stands adjourned until _____ *at* _____.

Permanent Organization: Second Meeting

❑ Opening the Meeting

Reading the Minutes. At the next meeting, the chair who was elected at the first meeting should call the meeting to order and ask the secretary to read the minutes. After the reading, the chair should ask if there are any corrections to the minutes and, if there are, should direct the secretary to make any such changes. Without asking for a motion, the chair might then state:

If there is no objection, the minutes will stand approved as corrected [or "as read" if no corrections were offered]. The next order of business is the adoption of the constitution. Will the chair of the constitution and bylaws committee please report?

See Chapter 3 for a description of the minutes and how they should be prepared.

Adjournment

Second Meeting

Reading Minutes

❑ Adoption of a Constitution

Amendments to Constitution. After the committee report is presented to the attendees, the chair would ask the committee chair or other designated person to read the constitution one article at a time. After each article is read, the chair should then ask:

Are there any amendments to this article?

After the reading of the third article, someone might state:

I move that the first sentence in Article III be amended to state: _____.

Each article, and any amendment that is proposed to it, must be discussed and opened to amendment by the attendees. (See the discussion of amending a document in Chapter 3.)

Finally, after going through the material article by article, the entire document must be offered as a whole for amendment. When there are no further amendments, a vote is taken on adopting the entire constitution, as amended.

Those in favor of adopting the constitution as amended say aye. Those opposed, no. The constitution has been adopted. I suggest that we now take a short recess so that those who want to become members of this organization can sign the constitution and pay the _____ initiation fee required by article _____. Only those signing will be entitled to vote on future matters.

After any required signatures or fees are collected and the recess is over, the chair can move on to the adoption of the bylaws, which should be handled article by article, the same as was done for the constitution.

Note: The attorney who is retained to handle incorporation or other matters for a new organization can provide sample constitutions for the group to consider and usually will prepare a draft of the proposed constitution for the organization.

❏ Election of Permanent Officers

Once the constitution and the bylaws are each adopted by the voting members, the organization assumes official status. A nominating committee can then be appointed to nominate permanent officers. Voting may be by ballot or by any other method allowed by the constitution and bylaws. (See the description of a nominating committee in the section "Assembly of Delegates," page 11, and see Chapter 3 for a description of the duties of the principal officers in an organization.)

Constitution, Bylaws, and Other Rules

❏ Constitution

Content of Articles. New organizations are advised to read copies of constitutions that have been prepared for and adopted by similar organizations. The number of articles (topics) in a constitution will vary depending on the type of organization and its needs. A small organization may require only a few basic articles, such as the following:

- Organization name
- Purpose of the organization
- Nature of the membership
- Required officers and elections
- Required meetings
- Procedure for amending the document

Additional articles might cover committees and an executive board or any other topic pertinent to the organization.

Amendment of the Constitution. Because a constitution contains only fundamental information, the organization should make it very difficult for the members to amend it. For example, the amendment procedure might specify that there must be previous notice to the members and a two-thirds (rather than a majority) vote for adoption of any amendment.

❏ Bylaws

Content of the Bylaws. The bylaws commonly provide greater detail about the organization's operations, its members, and the various rules it must follow. Some organizations put the rules of order and standing rules in two separate documents apart from the bylaws. Others include both types of rules within the bylaws. The articles in the bylaws will include details and instructions concerning topics such as the following:

- Membership requirements and qualifications
- Duties of officers
- Duties of the executive board (if any)
- Committees and their responsibilities
- Meetings (type, frequency, location, etc.)
- Required meeting notices
- Quorum requirements
- Elections and nominations
- Designation of the fiscal year
- Standing rules
- Rules of order and parliamentary authority
- Other rules written by the organization
- Amendment procedure and procedure for suspension of the rules

Other articles may be added as needed. *(Note:* The organization's attorney can provide sample bylaws and will usually prepare a draft of the proposed bylaws for the organization.)

Rules in the Bylaws. The rules in the bylaws should include all of those that are too important for the officers or directors to change on their own without giving prior notice to the members and without allowing the members to vote on the proposed change.

Article on Parliamentary Authority. After carefully reviewing books on parliamentary law or practice, such as *The New Robert's Rules of Order* (New American Library), based on General Robert's 1893 rules of order (see Chapter 1), an organization should add the following rule to its bylaws (in the article discussing its selected parliamentary authority):

The rules contained in ＿＿＿＿＿ shall govern the organization in all cases to which they are applicable and in which they are not inconsistent with the bylaws of this organization.

❑ Other Rules

Rules of Order. Rules of order pertain to the orderly transaction of business at a meeting. The rules of order found in a book on parliamentary law or procedure are usually more than adequate for an ordinary organization, although a group may want to add or substitute its own rules in certain instances. Those written by the organization in addition to or substituted for those in the selected parliamentary authority may be prepared in a separate document (cross-referenced in the bylaws) called "Rules of Order."

The rules of order, like the bylaws, should provide for its own amendment and suspension. Most complete texts on parliamentary law and procedure explain how to do this.

Standing Rules. Permanent resolutions (rules) that are binding on the organization until rescinded or modified may be included as an article in the bylaws. But they are sometimes provided as a separate document entitled "Standing Rules."

Standing rules can be adopted by a majority vote at any meeting. No previous notice is required, and members may terminate one or more of them at any future session. They should include only rules that are properly subject to the will of the majority at any meeting and must not include any rule that would be in conflict with the constitution, bylaws, or rules of order.

3 Officers and Committees

Duties of the Officers

❏ President

Principal Duties. The presiding officer is often referred to as the chair or chairman, unless an organization's constitution requires a different title, such as president. The duties of a chair include the following:

- Opening a meeting or session at the required time and calling a meeting to order
- Announcing business in the appropriate order
- Stating and putting to a vote any motions that are made
- Announcing the results of a vote
- Enforcing the rules of order on all occasions and, as a last resort, adjourning a meeting when disorder is so great that order can no longer be restored
- Deciding all questions of order, subject to an appeal by any two members of the organization
- Informing the attendees about a point of order and practice when necessary or when called on to do so
- Signing (authenticating) acts, orders, and proceedings (minutes) of the group
- Representing the group at all times and abiding by its rules

When the Chair May Vote. The chair may vote when voting is done by ballot but, otherwise, only when the vote would change the outcome. When voting by ballot, the chair must vote before the tellers begin counting the votes. If the count has started, the chair must ask for the permission of the assembly.

When a Chair Pro Tem Is Needed. A chair must know when to step down and let someone else temporarily assume the position.

- For the sake of objectivity, if a motion refers to the chair, he or she shouldn't put the motion to a vote. Either the secretary or the person making the motion should handle the voting.
- If a chair has to leave and no vice presidents are present, the chair may appoint another person as chair pro tem. The appointee may then serve as chair until the meeting is adjourned, unless the group wants to elect another chair pro tem before adjournment occurs.
- If any vice presidents are there, however, the first one on the list should be asked to fill in.
- Even if a chair expects to be absent from a future meeting, the appointment of a chair pro tem must wait until that meeting. If no vice presidents are present, the secretary or, in the secretary's absence, another member should call the meeting to order and ask for nominations for chair pro tem. The elected nominee would serve to the end of the session or until the regular chair returned. Again, if vice presidents were there, the first one on the list would be asked to assume the position of chair pro tem.
- Although a chair may ask an attendee to take over temporarily so that he or she may participate in the debate, the appearance of partisanship is not advisable, and this should never be done when the members object to it. As a rule, the chair should remain objective and not interject personal opinions on matters being discussed by the group.

The Chair and Parliamentary Usage. The chair must be very familiar with parliamentary practice and strictly follow the rules of the organization's adopted parliamentary author-

Chair Pro Tem

Chair's Procedure

ity (see Chapter 2). When an improper motion is made, for example, the chair shouldn't simply rule it out of order but should explain what the proper wording would be. (See Chapter 5 for a discussion of motions and the proper way to state them.)

Common sense is important, too, and with a small or very informal group, the chair need not insist on formal motions for routine matters such as approving the minutes. He or she can simply state:

If there is no objection, the minutes will stand approved as read [*or "as corrected"*].

Maintaining Order. To control others, a chair must first control himself or herself. An emotional chair might incite others to disruptive behavior.

Sometimes attendees try to obstruct the meeting proceedings or defeat the objectives of a meeting by making motions that are intended merely to delay action. The chair may refuse to entertain a dilatory (delaying) motion, although the opposition might then appeal the decision. However, if a majority sustains the chair's decision, he or she can also refuse to entertain any further appeals that are part of the opposition's efforts to obstruct proceedings. But a chair must never use the option of refusing to entertain a motion or an appeal when the attendees are sincere and aren't trying to obstruct the proceedings.

The chair is required to enforce any decision or rule of a group specifying that someone may not remain in the meeting, even if force is required to remove the person. An organization may not only expel someone but may investigate the character of a member. If the organization holds a "trial," it shouldn't be scheduled at the same meeting at which charges are brought.

Some groups have a standing committee to report any disciplinary cases that arise. Refer to a complete text of *Robert's Rules of Order* for further information on legal rights of assemblies to punish members, or consult an attorney if you have any doubts.

See Chapter 4 for details on the proper response of the

chair when someone is introducing business at a meeting or when members are engaged in debate.

❑ Vice President

Principal Duties. The vice president, or vice chairman, may have few or many duties, depending on the assignments made by the board of directors or specified in the bylaws. Sometimes the vice president serves as chair of certain committees and assists the president in carrying out his or her responsibilities. When present at a meeting, the vice president assumes the position of chair when the president is absent. In some organizations, the vice president is a top contender for the presidency when the president's term is over.

❑ Secretary

Principal Duties. The secretary, who is called the "clerk" or "recording secretary" in some organizations, keeps all official documents of the organization, such as the constitution, bylaws, rules of order, and property records. He or she is often required to sign all important papers along with the president and serves on the executive board or committee (if any), which usually consists of the president, vice president(s), secretary, and treasurer. Occasionally, the secretary also serves as treasurer, when the two positions are combined as secretary–treasurer.

The secretary usually sits near the chair at meetings and, when the chair is absent and no vice president is present, calls the meeting to order and presides until the group elects a chair pro tem. But the most important duty of the secretary is the recording, preparation, and maintenance of the minutes of each meeting.

Content of the Minutes. Since the minutes represent the official record of the organization's decisions, transactions, and operations, they must be completely accurate and unbiased. The secretary, therefore, must strictly observe the following code of conduct in preparing the minutes:

Vice President's Duties

Secretary's Duties

Minutes' Content

- Never interject personal opinions, whether flattering or unflattering.
- Always report only precise facts of the meeting proceedings, without subjective or personal interpretation of or judgment about anyone's statements or actions.
- Always report all sides of each debate without indication of personal or factional criticism or support for any side or any person's position.
- Never state as a fact something that has not been proved and is, therefore, only an opinion or allegation.
- Never make a statement that could be interpreted as an accusation of someone's criminal intent or action.
- Always attach to the minutes important correspondence and documents that are referenced in the minutes (except in the case of something such as classified material), particularly if the material is associated with a dispute and even if it points out questionable statements or actions of members of the board.
- Never omit information or alter a statement in an attempt to mislead others.
- Never use the minutes to develop an argument to hide inappropriate action by or a mistake of the board or any members of the board.
- Never refuse to correct inaccurate, misleading, subjective, or libelous statements in the minutes.
- Always refer to all authors when making references to multiauthor letters or documents, or refer to the first-named author on the document and add "et al." (and others); do not pick a name that appears in the middle of the list on the document, even if you believe that person is the principal author.

Subjective, personal attitudes about people or issues must never cause the secretary to slant the writing so that it will cast a person or an issue in a bad light. In regard to writing style, the qualities of total objectivity, fairness, honesty, and accuracy are far more important than brilliant prose.

Format of the Minutes. Minutes are usually taken by hand, with a backup tape recording. They should be prepared as

Minutes' Format

soon as possible after the meeting, signed by the secretary and president, and filed in the book of minutes. Even if a computer file is maintained, a hard copy should be printed out for the minutes book. The same is true if an alphabetical index of subjects is maintained; each time the index is updated by adding new topics, a revised copy should be printed out and filed at the front of the book of minutes.

The heading on the first page of the minutes should contain the organization's name, the type of meeting, and the date.

ABC CLUB OF AMERICA

Board of Directors
Special Meeting
January 3, 19--

The subheadings may all be in a column to the left of the text paragraphs (side subheading) or in the same column as the text just above the appropriate paragraphs (top-style subheading). Very long minutes are usually single spaced; short minutes are frequently double spaced. The following are examples of subheadings in formal minutes (typed in all capitals or with important words capitalized):

TIME AND PLACE
PRESIDING OFFICER; SECRETARY
ROLL CALL
NOTICE OF MEETING
PROOF OF NOTICE
INSPECTORS OF ELECTION
RESOLUTIONS
ADJOURNMENT

Examples of subheadings in informal minutes are:

CALL TO ORDER
READING OF MINUTES
FINANCIAL REPORTS

PROJECT X
ADJOURNMENT

The first paragraph of informal minutes (illustrated here with a top-style subheading) might read as follows:

CALL TO ORDER

A special meeting of the Board of Directors of the ABC Club of America was called to order at 2:30 p.m., August 6, 19--, at the New Motel Conference Room, 801 First Street, Arlington, Virginia 22209. The presiding officer was Jane Smith. A quorum was present, including the following (alphabetically): Nora Cross, Lynda Jamison, Daniel Johnson, Jane Smith, Timothy Snow, and Henry Stiles.

The conclusion of formal minutes (illustrated here with side subheadings) might look like this:

ADJOURNMENT   No other business coming before the meeting, it was thereupon adjourned at 4:05 p.m.

_____   _____

Secretary   President

The formality of statements depends on the group, but resolutions must always be reported verbatim:

RESOLVED, That _____.

Discussions, however, can be summarized in informal meetings:

The matter of enlarging the parking lot was considered, and it was unanimously agreed that the project should be discussed further at the next quarterly meeting.

In formal settings, the names of people making and seconding motions should be reported. In an informal setting, they are often omitted:

It was moved [by _____], seconded [by _____], and passed unanimously that the project to enlarge the parking lot be placed on the agenda at the next quarterly meeting.

❑ Treasurer

Principal Duties. In many organizations, the treasurer maintains the organization's checking and savings accounts and checkbooks, pays bills, assists the budget committee and auditors, and prepares financial reports, which are presented at board meetings and other organizational meetings.

In a small organization, the treasurer may also do the bookkeeping. In a larger organization, the treasurer may work with an outside bookkeeper or accountant. Often, the constitution and bylaws require that the treasurer be bonded (this may be required for all officers and directors).

Accounting and Financial Reporting. The complexity and detail required in financial reports depends on the organization. In many cases, all that is required is to report:

- The amount on hand at the beginning of the period in question
- The amount received since the close of the previous period
- The total amount paid since the close of the previous period
- The balance on hand

Organizations that have in-house or outside computerized accounting operations would follow the format of the software they are using. To avoid problems later, a new organization should check with an accountant or the intended auditor for formats that will satisfy accounting requirements of the auditors and the Internal Revenue Service, as well as satisfy any requirements of the constitution and bylaws.

Treasurer's Duties

Financial Reports

Treasurers and other persons who pay bills should collect receipts and vouchers to back up each payment or reimbursement that occurs. If you do the bookkeeping, follow the approved rules of cash or accrual accounting and always have the books audited by a qualified outside accountant or auditing firm. It is improper for the treasurer (or a personal friend of the treasurer) to act as auditor.

Collection of Monies. Organizations that collect dues should specify that payments be sent to the organization's business office or, if none exists, should make arrangements for a bank or other authorized firm to collect and deposit the monies. Funds should *never* be sent to a treasurer's personal residence, where safeguards are difficult to apply, where it is not possible to keep organizational funds and records fully apart from those of the household, and where the residence is not generally open to the public and all other members as a business office would be.

Committee Structure

❑ Purpose of Committees

Organizations form committees to handle special assignments or transact business pertaining to some aspect of their operations, such as budgeting, social events, elections, buildings and grounds maintenance, and meetings.

❑ Committee Members

Although in a very small group the board of directors might simply appoint one of its members to oversee a particular function, in a larger organization the chair might appoint or the members might elect several interested persons to serve on each committee. Each committee, in turn, might appoint its own subcommittee to focus on certain parts of its assigned work.

Ex-officio Members. An *ex-officio* member of a committee or a board is a member by virtue of holding another office.

Money Collection

Purpose   Committees

Members

Ex officio Members

Some bylaws state that the president, for example, is ex-officio a member of every committee in the organization. The president would not, however, be counted as a member in determining a quorum. An ex-officio member who is an officer of another organization still has the privileges of membership but is not under the authority of the organization that formed the committee.

Size. Committees range in size from a committee of one to a committee of the whole (the entire assembly). A committee formed to take action should be small and consist of only a few people who support the proposed action. A committee set up for deliberation or investigation, however, should be large and should have members that represent all of the main views in an organization.

❑ Selecting a Committee Chair

How to Select a Committee Chair. A committee chair may be appointed by the organization's presiding officer (chair) or may be elected by the voting members before the rest of the committee is selected. Or someone may make a motion that the group's presiding officer appoint the entire committee consisting of a certain number of people.

In that case, the first person named to be on the committee would become the committee chair. In the absence of that person, the next individual would become the chair, and so on. The committee, however, may elect its own chair if the organization has not already appointed someone. At its first meeting, the committee usually appoints or elects one of its members to serve as secretary.

What to Tell the New Chair. The secretary of the main assembly should immediately notify a selected committee chair of the following:

- Names of the committee members
- The matter referred to the committee (its assigned work)
- Instructions from the main assembly or the board of directors

Committee Meetings

❏ Rules That Apply to Committees

Calling Meetings. The committee chair may call a meeting or any two members may do so if the chair is absent or declines to call the meeting.

Difference Between Committee and Assembly Rules. In general, the rules of the organization apply to the committee and the conduct of its members. But unlike the chair of the main assembly, the committee chair takes an active part in meeting debate and discussion. Also, a motion in committee proceedings does not require a second, and members in a small committee do not stand to address the committee chair or make a motion.

Although formal motions need not be used in a small committee, the committee chair should ask for a vote on all matters. *(Note:* A vote may be reconsidered *only* when every member who voted with the majority is present at the time someone makes a motion to Reconsider. See Chapter 5 for a description of this motion.)

Unlike a main assembly, a committee has no authority to punish its members for disorderly conduct. But it can report the behavior to the main assembly. To do this, there must be general consent from the committee or a committee report must be prepared.

❏ When a Committee Concludes Its Work

Motion to Rise. When a committee finishes its assigned business, one of its members should make a motion for the committee to Rise and for the chair (or some designated person) to report to the main assembly. (In a committee, the motion to Rise is the same as the motion to Adjourn in the main assembly.) As soon as a committee that was appointed for a single special task has completed its business and the assembly has received its report, it ceases to exist.

Committee Meetings

Called Meetings

Committee Rules

Motion to Rise

Adjournment

Adjournment. A committee that adjourns without setting a time for another meeting can be called together again by the committee chair or any other two members, the same as with the first meeting. If it adjourns to meet at a certain time and place, it is a good idea to notify any members who were absent.

Committees of a Deliberative Assembly

❑ Types of Committees

Types of Committees

A *deliberative assembly*—a group of people meeting to discuss something and decide on a course of action for the group—may use one or all of the following three types of committees:

- *Standing committee:* A permanent committee required by the bylaws or one appointed for a specific session or a designated time, such as a year
- *Select committee:* A temporary committee appointed for a special purpose, such as to investigate a particular problem
- *Committee of the whole:* The entire assembly

❑ Matters Referred to a Committee

Committee Documents

Drafting and Amending Documents. Committees that are formed to prepare a report on some matter should meet as soon as possible to begin work. If a resolution or document has been referred to a committee, the committee chair should read each paragraph, article, section, or other division and pause after each one to allow amendments to be offered and voted on.

Amendments

If a committee receives from the main assembly a document that has already been prepared, it can only vote on the amendments; it can't adopt the entire document that was referred to it. The main assembly must do that. If the committee drafts the document from scratch, however, at the conclusion of all paragraph-by-paragraph readings and amendments, the committee would vote to adopt the entire report, with amendments incorporated, before submitting it to the assembly for final adoption.

Note: The same paragraph-by-paragraph reading and amendment procedure applies whether an already-prepared document is referred to the committee for further work or whether the committee must draft the document from scratch.

Submission Format. If a document is referred to the committee by the main assembly, it must return the document intact, with the proposed amendments written on a *separate* sheet of paper. But if the entire document is drafted by the committee, it should incorporate any amendments into the text that it drafts and submit the amended text as a complete document.

❑ Executive Session

A deliberative assembly that wants to keep secret all or part of its proceedings may go into executive session under certain circumstances. In ordinary organizations, matters pertaining to discipline, the investigation of a member's character, and other sensitive topics should be discussed in a closed session. An organization does not have the right to make public information regarding the character of any of its members or any charge brought forth at an organization's trial. The public release of such details, in fact, could constitute libel. The minutes of an executive session should be prepared apart from the regular minutes and read only in another executive session.

A motion to go into executive session is one of privilege that must be considered immediately:

I move that the open portion of this meeting be declared ended and that our guests now be excused so that the board may consider _____ in a closed session.

Organizations should not, however, use the executive session with nonsensitive matters merely as an excuse to exclude members who otherwise have a right to attend the organization's meetings. Public boards, commissions, and committees, in particular, must carefully weigh the sensitivity of proceedings against the public's right to information. Consult an attorney when in doubt. (Information about a citizen's right to federal agency records is described in *Your Right to Federal Records*. This booklet discusses both the Freedom of Information Act and the Privacy Act.)

❑ Committee of the Whole

Forming a Committee of the Whole. If an assembly wants to consider a subject but does *not* want to refer it to a committee, it can turn itself into a committee of the whole and act with the freedom of an ordinary committee. The entire group, then, would go to work the same as a small committee would do. If at any time it should want to return to the stricter rules of the main assembly, it can make a motion to Rise and report, and the committee of the whole will then automatically return to its status as the main assembly.

To form a committee of the whole, someone should make a motion as follows:

I move that the assembly now resolve itself into a committee of the whole to consider _____.

Handling Motions and Debate. The only motions in order in a committee of the whole are those to Amend, to adopt, and to Rise and report. The only way to close or limit debate in a committee of the whole is for the main assembly to vote beforehand that (a) the debate in the committee of the whole must cease at a certain time or (b) after a certain time no debate will be allowed except on new amendments. Also, some restrictions could be put on the number of arguments allowed or on the time allowed for each one.

When Business Is Finished. After a committee of the whole concludes its business, the presiding officer returns as chair of the main assembly. The chair of the committee of the whole can then inform him or her that:

Committee of the Whole

Motions and Debate

Reporting

The committee has completed the business referred to it, and I'm ready to make the report when the assembly is ready to receive it.

Minutes. The main assembly's secretary should take notes while the body is acting as a committee of the whole and give a memo of the proceedings to the committee for its use. These notes, however, are not included in the minutes of the main assembly.

Committee Reports

❏ Reporting to an Assembly

Heading of a Committee Report. A committee report usually has a heading such as this:

Report of the Rules Committee

of the ABC Club, Inc.

on the Review of Its Standing Rules

Opening and Closing of a Committee Report. Committee reports usually begin with something like this:

The committee on _____ respectfully reports that _____.

In addition to a report by a standing committee, a select committee, or a committee of the whole, a report by the minority of any committee may be prepared and presented. It might begin:

The undersigned, a minority of the committee on _____, respectfully report that _____.

Committee reports are usually signed only by the committee chair but may be signed by others in the committee who concur.

❏ Receiving a Report

Procedure in Receiving a Report. Receiving a report means that an assembly is agreeing to hear it, *not* to accept or adopt it and not to agree to its content. That comes later.

Most assemblies do not formally vote to receive a report unless someone insists on a motion. Otherwise, when the committee chair advises the main assembly chair that it is ready to report, and when the main assembly is ready to hear (receive) the report, the assembly chair simply asks the committee chair to read it and then deliver it to the assembly's secretary.

The person reading the amendments should explain the reason for them and go through all of them. After the presentation, the person reading might make a motion that the assembly adopt (or accept or agree to) the report. If there is a minority report, however, it is often read right after the committee's report. But it is not voted on unless someone makes a motion to substitute it for the committee's report.

❏ Adopting a Report

Adopting a Report That the Committee Has Drafted. After a report that a committee drafts has been read to the assembly and someone has made a motion to adopt (or accept or agree to) it, the motion is seconded. The report is then offered to the entire assembly for amendment, even though the committee that reported it may have just finished amending it.

The assembly chair should restate the motion that was made and seconded to adopt the report and then direct the assembly secretary or the committee member who has presented it to read each paragraph, article, section, or other separate division one at a time. After each item is read, the assembly chair should ask the assembly if there are any amendments to it. In this case, voting is put off until the end. That way, after each item has been amended, the document as a whole remains open to further amendment. Finally, when no one has any more amendments to offer, the entire report, as amended, is put to a vote.

Receiving Report

Adopting Report

Committee Draft

Adopting a Report That the Assembly Provides. If the assembly provides an already-drafted document and the committee merely amends it, the reporting committee member reads *only* the amendments of the committee, rather than the entire document, and makes a motion to the main assembly to adopt those amendments. After that motion is seconded, the amendments are read and offered one at a time for debate and further amendment. In this case, a vote is taken on adopting each amendment immediately after it has been debated and amended further. This procedure is followed for each succeeding amendment until completion. (New amendments by the assembly to the *document* aren't allowed at this time; only amendments to the committee's *amendments* are accepted.)

How to Adopt a Report Quickly. If a group wants to avoid the slow process of going through a document one item at a time, it can vote to suspend the rules (see Chapter 5) and adopt the report as amended by general consent.

Assembly Draft

Quick Adoption

4 Introduction of Business

The Agenda

❑ Order of Business

Business must be introduced at a meeting in an orderly fashion, following the topics listed on the agenda. Most organized groups have a format and standard order of business that is suitable for their purposes (study examples of agendas from previous meetings).

❑ Soliciting Topics

The chair or secretary may distribute a notice before the meeting stating that an agenda is being prepared and asking participants to submit items that they want to discuss at the meeting. Such matters are then added to the final version of the agenda, usually under the heading of old or new business.

Preliminary Topics. A preliminary agenda might have some or all of the following topics (the final version would add more detail as information is received).

- Call to order
- Reading, correction, and approval of previous minutes
- Officers' reports (e.g., treasurer)
- Executive committee report
- Standing committee reports (e.g., membership)
- Special committee reports (e.g., annual conference)
- Old business (unfinished from previous meeting)

- New business
- Announcements
- Adjournment

Introduction of Business

❏ How to Introduce Business at a Meeting

Motions and Reports. You can bring business before an assembled group in one of two ways:

- Make a motion that the assembly consider or act on something
- Present a report or other communication to the assembly

The chair may require that all principal motions (see Chapter 5 for a list), all amendments, and all committee instructions be in writing. Follow the form prescribed in your organization.

Planning What You Will Say. If you have something to say or a motion to make at a meeting, plan your remarks beforehand. Unless your comments will be very simple, write down what you want to say so that you don't have to rely on your memory in front of the assembly.

❏ Obtaining the Floor

Procedure. Before you can make a motion, present a report, or address the assembly, you must obtain the floor. To do this in a formal setting, you would stand and wait for the chair to recognize you. In a small, informal meeting, you can get the chair's attention in some other way, such as raising your hand.

After standing or making your intent known in another way, address the chair by title in a formal setting and, after being recognized, state your name (but don't interrupt someone else who is speaking, and sit down if the chair rises to speak before recognizing you):

Introducing Business

Planning Remarks

Obtaining Floor

Madam President

Mr. Chairman

❑ How to Make a Motion

Formal and informal motions. Informal motions are usually stated by using the word *move*.

I move that _____.

A more formal motion can be stated as a resolution.

I move that we adopt the following resolution: RESOLVED, That _____.

❑ The Chair's Duties

Recognizing Members. The chair should recognize someone trying to obtain the floor by announcing the person's name (if known) in a large assembly or, in a small group, perhaps by nodding at the person:

The chair recognizes Ms. McDermitt.

Guidelines for the Chair. Follow these guidelines in the introduction of business:

- If more than one person wants to speak, first recognize anyone who made a motion being discussed or who presented a report being discussed, unless he or she has already had the floor.
- Let people on both sides of an issue speak.
- Don't recognize someone who stood up and remained standing while someone else was speaking if a third person rises after the speaker is finished.
- Don't allow any interruptions when someone legitimately has the floor except in these circumstances (refer to Chapter 5 for descriptions of each motion):
  —To enter in the minutes a motion to Reconsider

—To allow a question of order
—To recognize an Objection to the Consideration of a Question
—To call for Orders of the Day
—To admit a Question of Privilege that requires immediate action

Seconding a Motion. If someone makes a motion that is in order (is proper) and is debatable (see Chapter 5), ask for a second if none is offered:

Is there a second to the motion to _____?

Members often respond by stating:

I second the motion.

In a large or formal meeting, however, where the members are unknown, those who speak should be asked to stand and give their names so that full information can be recorded in the minutes.

Yielding the Floor. After a motion has been properly made and seconded, no one should make another motion unless the first person decides to yield the floor. If that appears to be occurring, you might ask:

Will Mr. Jenkins yield the floor now?

A person who has the floor doesn't lose it by asking the secretary to read something, such as a report. As soon as the secretary is finished, the person submitting the material resumes the floor to make a motion that it be adopted. See Chapter 3 for a description of receiving and adopting a committee report. See the section "Precedence of Motions" in Chapter 5 for information about which motions can be made while another motion is pending.

Seconding Motions

Yielding Floor

❑ Modifying a Motion

Procedure. After a motion has been made and seconded, the chair states the motion again to the assembly before opening the matter to debate (discussion). Before the chair does this, however, the person who made the motion can quickly withdraw or modify it. After the chair has stated it, the person must get the consent of the assembly to do so.

Mr. Phillips: *I move that we adopt the Jordan Plan.*

Ms. Hendricks: *I second the motion.*

Mr. Phillips: *Before the chair reads the motion, I'd like to modify it to read: "I move that we adopt the Jordan Plan as revised on December 9, 19--."*

Ms. Hendricks: *I then withdraw my second.*

Chair: *Is there a second to Mr. Phillips's modified statement that _____?*

Mr. Harris: *I second the modified motion.*

Chair: *A motion to adopt the Jordan Plan as revised on December 9, 19--, has been made and seconded. Is there any discussion?* [*Or "The matter is now open to debate."*]

❑ Dividing a Motion

When to Divide a Motion. If a motion is particularly complicated, it may be simplified by dividing it into several simpler motions. To do this, someone should make a motion to Amend (divide) the motion into two or more individual motions and specify how the division would be made.

When Not to Divide a Motion. Each separate new motion must be something the assembly can act on independent of the other resulting new motion(s). Some things could not be acted on independently. For example, you could not logically divide a motion to strike out certain words and insert others.

If the motion to strike out some words passed but the motion to insert other words failed, the result would not make sense.

Rules of Debate

❏ How to Open Debate

The chair always opens debate by restating a motion that has been made and seconded (mentioning the members' names in a formal setting):

It has been moved [by _____] and seconded [by _____] that _____. Is there any discussion?

❏ Guidelines for the Chair

Follow these guidelines in conducting the discussion that follows a debatable motion:

- No one may speak more than twice on the same motion and only once on a question of order. *(Exception:* A member who presents a committee report is always allowed to close debate on that matter.)
- No one may speak a second time on a motion until everyone else who wants to speak has done so. *(Note:* Amending a motion changes it so that you would no longer be speaking on the original motion.)
- No one may speak more than ten minutes (or other specified time) without the permission of two-thirds of the assembly.
- No one who makes a motion may speak against it, but may vote against it.
- When an amendment is pending, the debate must be confined to that amendment unless a decision on the amendment effectively decides the entire main question.
- The chair may not close debate as long as anyone wants to speak. Even if a motion has been made and seconded to close the discussion and put the matter to a vote, and even after the yes portion of the voting procedure has

occurred—but before the no portion—a person still has the right to speak.

See Chapter 5 for information about which motions are debatable and which are amendable.

Voting Procedure

❑ How to Put a Motion to a Vote

What to Say. In a formal setting, the chair should stand to put a motion to a vote. In an informal setting, the chair usually remains seated. *(Note:* When addressing the assembly, the chair always refers to himself or herself as "the chair," never as "I.")

After a motion has been made and seconded and discussion appears to have ended, the chair should ask:

Is there any further discussion? Or: *Are you ready for the question?*

If no further debate is requested, the chair should again restate the motion and put it to a vote:

All those in favor of the motion to _____, say aye. Those opposed, no.

If the vote is taken by some other means, such as show of hands, ballots, or roll call (each member says yes or no when called), the chair should rephrase the statement to instruct the members on how to vote by that method, for example:

All those in favor of the motion to _____, please raise your hand. Those opposed, raise your hand.

Announcing the Results. Most motions require only a majority of votes cast to pass. (Chapter 5 lists those that require a two-thirds vote.) After the vote has been taken (and

Voting Procedure

Putting a Question

Announcing Results

counted, in the case of ballots or roll call), the chair should immediately announce the results:

The motion is carried. The _____ *is adopted.*

The no's have it. The motion has failed.

Even after the vote is announced, members may state that they doubt the vote or may call for a division of the motion. On a proposed division, the chair might respond:

A division has been called for. Those in favor please rise. Those opposed, rise.

Tellers. If tellers are appointed (at least two) for voting by ballot, they should be selected from both sides of an issue. The tellers would then distribute slips of paper on which members would write their votes. *(Note:* The chair may vote when this form of voting is used.) After the slips are collected, the tellers should count the ballots and report the results to the chair, who would immediately announce the results to the assembly.

Tellers

5 Motions

Classification of Motions

❏ General Classification

Motions, also referred to as *questions,* are proposals made before an organized meeting (assembly) for the members' consideration and action. *Robert's Rules of Order* classifies motions as follows:

- Privileged motions
- Incidental motions
- Subsidiary, or secondary, motions
- Main, or principal, motions

Privileged Motion. A *privileged motion,* the highest-ranking motion, is not related to the subject of matter of any motion currently being discussed but takes precedence over it. This type of motion may be used to bring about adjournment or recess, to set times for adjournment or for the next meeting, or to ask the chair to return to the specified order of business for a meeting (see the section "Orders of the Day," page 59). If no other business is currently before an assembly, a privileged motion is sometimes treated as a main motion and hence debated. (See the section "Debatable and Amendable Motions," page 49.)

Incidental Motion. An *incidental motion* is prompted by or arises from another motion and, therefore, has to be decided before action can be taken on the other motion. Two exceptions are that privileged motions must be decided before incidental motions, and incidental motions cannot be amended. A proposal to Withdraw a Motion, for example, would be an incidental motion prompted by or arising from the other motion.

Subsidiary, or Secondary, Motion. A *subsidiary motion* is one that is applied to another motion currently being considered as a means of disposing of the other motion. Someone might, for example, propose that an Appeal (the other motion) Lay on the Table (the subsidiary motion). Tabling the Appeal would dispose of it. You can use any subsidiary motion, except the one to Amend, when a lower-ranking motion is pending, but you cannot make a subsidiary motion when a higher-ranking motion is pending.

Main, or Principal, Motion. A *main motion* is a proposal made on any subject with the objective of introducing business to the members participating in a meeting. For example: "I move that we retain the firm of Arnold & Samuels to perform our annual audit." Contrary to what the name might suggest, a main motion is of lower rank than any motion in the other three categories (subsidiary, incidental, or privileged). Therefore, it yields to all other motions (the others must be handled first) and may not be made while one of the higher-ranking motions is before the assembly. (See the next section, "Precedence of Motions," for more about the rank of motions.)

Rules About Motions

❑ Precedence of Motions

When more than one motion arises, rules of precedence are applied to determine which motion takes precedence over the other motion, that is, which of two or more motions a group should consider first. *Robert's Rules of Order* ranks privileged motions first; incidental motions, second; subsidiary motions, third; and main motions, fourth.

Subsidiary Motion

Main Motion

Rules

Precedence

Motions Listed by Rank. Important privileged and subsidiary motions are listed below in order of precedence. For example, the privileged motion to Fix the Time to Which to Adjourn takes precedence over all other motions in that category (and in all other categories), and the motion to Adjourn takes precedence over all except the one to Fix the Time to Which to Adjourn. *(Note:* Individual incidental motions have no particular rank within that category.) In parliamentary practice, a higher-ranking motion must be disposed of before a lower-ranking motion can be considered. For a definition of each motion listed here, see the section "Use of Important Motions," page 52.

Privileged Motions (First Rank)
- Fix the Time to Which to Adjourn
- Adjourn
- Rise to Question of Privilege
- Call for Orders of the Day

Incidental Motions (Second Rank)
- Appeal
- Object to Consideration of a Question
- Read a Paper
- Point of Order
- Withdraw a Motion
- Suspend the Rules

Subsidiary Motions (Third Rank)
- Lay on the Table
- Call for the Previous Question
- Limit or Extend the Limits of Debate
- Postpone to a Certain Time
- Commit or Refer
- Amend
- Postpone Indefinitely

Main Motions (Fourth Rank)
- Any motion made to introduce business at a meeting

Various miscellaneous motions do not clearly fit into any of these four categories, for example:

- Take from the table
- Reconsider
- Rescind

❑ Motions Requiring Two-Thirds Vote

In determining the number of votes on a matter, blanks are never counted. A two-thirds vote, therefore, means two-thirds of the votes actually cast.

The bylaws of an organization should specify which types of decisions require a majority vote or a two-thirds vote. It also should specify whether a decision requires a two-thirds vote of the members present at a meeting or two-thirds of the entire membership of the organization.

Here are eight important motions requiring a two-thirds (rather than a mere majority) vote to be adopted.

- Amend the Rules (also requires previous notice)
- Suspend the Rules
- Make a Special Order
- Take up a Question Out of Its Proper Order
- Object to Consideration of a Question
- Extend the Limits of Debate
- Limit or Close Debate
- Call for the Previous Question

Debatable and Amendable Motions

The following motions are classified as debatable or undebatable motions and amendable or unamendable motions. Notice that in some cases a motion falls in both categories. Refer to the appropriate footnotes to this table for an explanation in such cases.

Two-Thirds Vote

Debatable, Amendable Motions

Debatable Motions	Can Amend	Cannot Amend
Adjourn, Fix the Time to Which to[1]	X	
Amend or Substitute	X	
Amend an Amendment		X
Amend the Rules	X	
Appeal[2]		X
Commit or Refer	X	
Postpone to a Certain Time[3]	X	
Postpone Indefinitely		X
Reconsider a Debatable Question		X
Rescind	X	
Special Order, Make a	X	

Undebatable Motions	Can Amend	Cannot Amend
Adjourn		X
Adjourn, Fix the Time to Which to[4]	X	
Appeal (relating to indecorum etc.)[5]		X
Call (a Member) to Order		X
Close Debate		X
Extend the Limits of Debate	X	
Lay on the Table		X
Limit Debate	X	

---

[1]Undebatable if made when another motion is before the assembly.

[2]A motion to Appeal is undebatable only when relating to indecorum, to transgressions of the rules of speaking, to the priority of business, or when made while the Previous Question is pending. When an Appeal is debatable, only one speech from each member is permitted. On a tie vote, the decision of the chair is sustained.

[3]Allows but limited debate on the propriety of the postponement.

[4]See note 1.

[5]See note 2.

Undebatable Motions	Can Amend	Cannot Amend
Object to Consideration of a Question[6]		X
Orders of the Day		X
Postpone to a Certain Time[7]	X	
Previous Question		X
Privilege, Questions of		X
Reading Papers		X
Reconsider an Undebatable Question		X
Request to Continue Speaking after Indecorum		X
Rise (in committee = Adjourn)		X
Suspend the Rules		X
Take from the Table		X
Take up a Question Out of Its Proper Order		X
Withdraw a Motion		X

❑ Motions That Open Main Question to Debate

Of the debatable motions, these four will open to debate the entire merits of the main question that is before the assembly:

- Commit or Refer
- Postpone Indefinitely
- Reconsider a Debatable Question
- Rescind

❑ Motions That Cannot Be Reconsidered

The following eight motions cannot be reconsidered:

- Adjourn
- Call (a Member) to Order

---

[6]The objection can be made only when the question is first introduced, before debate.

[7]See note 3.

Open Debate

Cannot Reconsider

- Call for Orders of the Day
- Lay on the Table
- Reconsider a Debatable Question
- Rise (in committee = Adjourn)
- Suspend the Rules
- Take from the Table

❏ Motions That Need No Second

These three motions need not be seconded:

- Call (a Member) to Order
- Object to Consideration of a Question
- Call for Orders of the Day

❏ Motions in Order When Another Has the Floor

The following five motions are in order even though someone else may have the floor:

- Appeal
- Call (a Member) to Order
- Object to Consideration of a Question
- Call for Orders of the Day
- Reconsider a Question (can be moved and entered on record when another has the floor but cannot interrupt business before the assembly; must be made on day, or day after, original vote is taken by one voting with presiding side)

Use of Important Motions

The following summaries of important motions are listed alphabetically for convenience. For expanded information on a particular motion or details concerning exceptions to the rules given here, consult a complete parliamentary text. (See the section "Precedence of Motions," page 47, for the rank of motions.)

❑ Adjourn

The motion to Adjourn is used to dismiss an assembly.

FORM: *I move that we adjourn.*

* Privileged motion
* Must be seconded
* Cannot be debated
* Cannot be amended
* Cannot be reconsidered
* Requires a majority vote
* Not in order when someone else has the floor

The motion to Recess (see definition in Chapter 2) is similar to a motion to Adjourn except that it can be amended.

In a committee, when all assigned business is finished, the correct motion is to Rise and report, which is equivalent to the motion to Adjourn in a main assembly.

❑ Adjourn, Fix the Time to Which to

The motion to Fix the Time to Which to Adjourn is used to set the time (or time, date, and place if appropriate) for a future meeting.

FORM: *I move that when the assembly adjourns, it adjourn to meet at _____ on _____ in _____.*

* Privileged motion
* Must be seconded
* Cannot be debated
* Time and place can be amended
* May be reconsidered
* Requires a majority vote
* Not in order when someone else has the floor

Adjourn

Fix Time to Which to Adjourn

❑ Amend

The motion to Amend is used to change or revise something.

FORM: *I move that we amend the motion by striking out the words _____ and inserting the words _____.*

- Subsidiary motion
- Must be seconded
- Can be debated
- Can be amended
- Can be reconsidered
- Requires a majority vote
- Not in order when someone else has the floor

The motion to Substitute is the same as the motion to Amend.

❑ Amend an Amendment

The motion to Amend an Amendment is used to change or revise an amendment to something.

FORM: *I move that we amend the amendment by adding the words _____.*

- Subsidiary motion
- Must be seconded
- Can be debated
- Cannot be amended
- Can be reconsidered
- Requires a majority vote
- Not in order when someone else has the floor

❑ Amend the Rules

The motion to Amend the Rules is used to change or revise the rules of order to which the meeting is subject.

FORM: *I move that we amend rule 17 in the Rules of Order by* _____ .

- Main motion
- Must be seconded
- Can be debated
- Can be amended
- Negative vote can be reconsidered
- Requires a two-thirds vote
- Not in order when someone else has the floor

❑ Appeal Relating to Decorum

Some motions to Appeal—to question or object to something—relate to indecorum, to transgression of the rules of speaking, or to the priority of business.

FORM: *I appeal from the decision of the chair.*

- Incidental motion
- Must be seconded
- Cannot be debated
- Cannot be amended
- Can be reconsidered
- Requires a majority vote
- In order when someone else has the floor

❑ Appeal Relating to Other Matters

The motion to Appeal in other cases is used in the same way—to question or object to something.

FORM: *I appeal from the decision of the chair.*

- Incidental motion
- Must be seconded
- Can be debated
- Cannot be amended
- Can be reconsidered
- Requires a majority vote
- In order when someone else has the floor

Appeal—Decorum

Other Appeal

❑ Call (a Member) to Order

The Call to Order, not to be confused with the expression used to open a meeting, may be the statement of a member pointing out the violation of another member or a statement of the chair used to instruct someone to conform to the rules.

FORM: *I rise to a point of order* (member). *I call the member to order* (chair).

- Incidental motion
- Does not have to be seconded
- Cannot be debated
- Cannot be amended
- Cannot be reconsidered
- Does not require a vote
- In order when someone else has the floor

❑ Close Debate

The motion to Close Debate brings discussion of a motion to a close. An assembly can also adopt an order to limit debate in terms of the number of debates allowed, the length of time allowed per debate, or the specific time when all debate will cease. These motions will effectively close debate: to Limit Debate, to Lay on the Table, to Object to the Consideration of a Question, and to Call for the Previous Question. See the descriptions of these motions in this chapter.

FORM: *I move that we close debate and vote immediately on the pending question.*

- Subsidiary motion
- Must be seconded
- Cannot be debated
- Cannot be amended
- Can be reconsidered
- Requires a two-thirds vote
- Not in order when someone else has the floor

❑ Commit or Refer

The motion to Commit or Refer is used to assign some task to a few members, such as a committee.

FORM: *I move that _____ be referred to a committee of three to be appointed by the chair.*

- Subsidiary motion
- Must be seconded
- Can be debated
- Can be amended
- Can be reconsidered
- Requires a majority vote
- Not in order when someone else has the floor

❑ Extend the Limits of Debate

The motion to Extend the Limits of Debate is used to allow further discussion that will exceed specified limits on debate in terms of number or length of speeches.

FORM: *I move that we increase the number of speeches to five and that the time for each speech be increased to ten minutes.*

- Subsidiary motion
- Must be seconded
- Cannot be debated
- Can be amended
- Can be reconsidered
- Requires a two-thirds vote
- Not in order when someone else has the floor

❑ Lay on the Table

The motion to Lay on the Table (table something) is used to put business aside temporarily and hold it for later discussion.

Commit, Refer

Extend Debate

Lay on Table

FORM: *I move that this matter be laid on the table* [or *tabled*].

• Subsidiary motion
• Must be seconded
• Cannot be debated
• Cannot be amended
• Cannot be reconsidered
• Requires a majority vote
• Not in order when someone else has the floor

❑ Limit Debate

The motion to Limit Debate is used to set a limit on the number of speakers and the time that each may speak.

FORM: *I move that debate be limited to six members, three on each side of the issue, and five minutes for each member.*

• Subsidiary motion
• Must be seconded
• Cannot be debated
• Can be amended
• Can be reconsidered
• Requires a two-thirds vote
• Not in order when someone else has the floor

❑ Object to Consideration of a Question

The motion Objecting to Consideration of a Question is used to discourage the discussion of a matter believed to be irrelevant, unprofitable, or contentious.

FORM: *I object to the consideration of the question.*

• Incidental motion
• Does not have to be seconded
• Cannot be debated
• Cannot be amended
• Negative vote can be reconsidered

- Requires a two-thirds vote against consideration
- In order when someone else has the floor (before debate)

❑ Orders of the Day

The motion calling for Orders of the Day is used to force the assembly to return to its scheduled program.

FORM: *I call for the orders of the day.*

- Privileged motion
- Does not have to be seconded
- Cannot be debated
- Cannot be amended
- Cannot be reconsidered
- No vote required to return to Orders of the Day; requires a two-thirds vote against returning to defeat call
- In order when someone else has the floor

❑ Postpone to a Certain Time

The motion to Postpone to a Certain Time is used to establish a time when a particular subject must be considered.

FORM: *I move that this matter be postponed to* _____.

- Subsidiary motion
- Must be seconded
- Can be debated
- Can be amended
- Can be reconsidered
- Requires a majority vote
- Not in order when someone else has the floor

❑ Postpone Indefinitely

The motion to Postpone Indefinitely is used by members opposing a motion in order to open the main question to debate. They can then find out how strongly the other side feels before the main question is put to a vote.

FORM: *I move that this matter be postponed indefinitely.*

- Subsidiary motion
- Must be seconded
- Can be debated
- Cannot be amended
- Affirmative vote can be reconsidered
- Requires a majority vote
- Not in order when someone else has the floor

❑ Previous Question

Although it may not be clear from its name, the motion calling for the Previous Question is used to bring debate on a current motion to a close and order an immediate vote.

FORM: *I move* [or *call for*] *the previous question.*

- Subsidiary motion
- Must be seconded
- Cannot be debated
- Cannot be amended
- Can be reconsidered
- Requires a two-thirds vote
- Not in order when someone else has the floor

❑ Priority of Business

Some members at a meeting might like to skip less important matters and consider more urgent topics first. To transact business out of the specified order, however, it is necessary to suspend the rules. Or individual matters can be tabled, one after another, until the urgent matter comes up. But an entire category, such as all committee reports, cannot be tabled. In general, it is improper to put aside anything except the question currently being considered. See the sections "Lay on the Table," page 57, and "Suspend the Rules," page 63.

❑ Privilege, Questions of

Some matters pertain to the rights and privileges of the assembly or any of its members. These Questions of Privilege fall in the category of privileged motions. Examples of points pertaining to rights and privileges are disorderly conduct or charges brought against a member. The purpose of calling for a point of privilege is to get the attention of the chair immediately, to ask the chair a question, or to make some other point that cannot wait. Questions of privilege are usually decided informally by the chair without a formal motion or vote.

FORM: *I rise to a question of privilege.*

❑ Reading Papers

The motion to Read a Paper is used to request that a paper brought before an assembly be read once before a vote on it is taken.

FORM: *I move that _____ be permitted to read _____.*

- Incidental motion
- Must be seconded
- Cannot be debated
- Cannot be amended
- Can be reconsidered
- Requires a majority vote
- Not in order when someone else has the floor

❑ Reconsider a Question

The motion to Reconsider a Question is used to bring a previously decided matter before the assembly again. A vote to Reconsider a Question must be made on the day or the day after the original vote was taken and by someone who voted with the prevailing side.

Question of Privilege

Reading Papers

Reconsider Question

FORM: *I move that we reconsider the vote on the motion to* _____.

- Motion to bring back another question previously decided
- Must be seconded
- Opens main question to debate if the main question is debatable
- Cannot be amended
- Cannot be reconsidered
- Requires a majority vote
- In order when someone else has the floor before that person begins to speak

❑ Request to Continue Speaking after Indecorum

The motion to Continue Speaking after Indecorum is used to get permission from the assembly to continue a discussion after being called to order for making improper remarks. The chair may put the question to a vote without a motion, or someone else may make a motion.

FORM: *I move that* _____ *be permitted to continue speaking.*

- Incidental motion
- Must be seconded if in the form of a motion
- Cannot be debated
- Cannot be amended
- Can be reconsidered
- Requires a majority vote
- Not in order when someone else has the floor

❑ Rescind

The motion to Rescind is used to annul a previous action when it is too late to use the motion to Reconsider.

FORM: *I move that the motion to* _____ *adopted on* _____ *be rescinded.*

- Motion to annul the vote on another question previously decided
- Must be seconded
- Can be debated
- Can be amended
- Negative vote can be reconsidered
- Requires a majority vote if previous notice is given; two-thirds vote if no notice was given
- Not in order when someone else has the floor

❏ Special Order

The motion to create a Special Order is used to suspend all of the rules of an assembly that would interfere with considering a question at a specified time. Someone might move, for example, to postpone considering a matter until a certain time and make it a special order for that time. It would then take precedence over all other topics on the agenda at that time.

FORM: *I move that _____ be made a special order for 1:30 this afternoon.*

- Subsidiary or main motion
- Must be seconded
- Can be debated
- Can be amended
- Can be reconsidered
- Requires a two-thirds vote
- Not in order when someone else has the floor

❏ Suspend the Rules

The motion to Suspend the Rules is used to enable an assembly to act on a matter that would otherwise be prohibited by the rules. It must not, however, be a matter in conflict with the constitution or bylaws (the bylaws usually have a provision regarding its own suspension).

FORM: *I move that we suspend the rules that interfere with _____.*

- Incidental motion
- Must be seconded
- Cannot be debated
- Cannot be amended
- Cannot be reconsidered
- Requires a two-thirds vote
- Not in order when someone else has the floor

❏ Take from the Table

The motion to Take from the Table is used to bring back to the floor for consideration a question that was previously tabled.

FORM: *I move that the motion _____ be taken from the table.*

- Motion to bring back previously tabled motion
- Must be seconded
- Cannot be debated
- Cannot be amended
- Cannot be reconsidered
- Requires a majority vote
- Not in order when someone else has the floor

❏ Take Up a Question Out of Order

To transact business out of order, you must suspend the rules or table matters, one at a time, to move the proceedings to the topic of interest. See the explanation under the section "Priority of Business," page 60.

FORM: *I move that we suspend the rules and take up _____.*

❏ Withdraw a Motion

The motion to Withdraw a Motion is used to remove another motion from further consideration and to prevent a vote on it. The chair may state that it is withdrawn if there is

no objection. But if someone objects, a motion must be made
and voted on.

FORM: *I'd like to withdraw my motion. I move that
_____ be allowed to withdraw his motion.*

- Incidental motion
- Must be seconded
- Cannot be debated
- Cannot be amended
- Negative vote can be reconsidered
- Requires a majority vote
- Not in order when someone else has the floor

Glossary

abstain. Refraining from voting.

accept a report. To *adopt* a report. See Chapter 3.

acclamation. An affirmative vote by overwhelming applause or cheers.

ad hoc. Formed or used for immediate, temporary needs, such as a *special committee.*

adjourn. To end a *meeting.* See also *recess.*

adjourned meeting. The continuation of a *meeting* that was adjourned until a later time but before the next regular *session.*

adopt. A decision to accept a *motion* and put it into effect. Used interchangeably with accept, agree to, and approve. See Chapter 3.

agenda. A list of things to be considered or done at a *meeting;* the order of *business* at a meeting. See Chapter 4; see also *orders of the day.*

agree to. See *adopt.*

amend. To change or modify a *motion.* See Chapter 5.

amendment. The proposed alteration of a *motion.*

annual meeting. The yearly *meeting* of stockholders or members of an organization, including the election of officers and directors.

appeal. To question or disagree with a decision made by the *chair.* See Chapter 5.

approve. See *adopt.*

assembly. A body of persons or members of an organization gathered for deliberation and action.

audioconference. An electronic *meeting* conducted by telephone (voice only). See also *videoconference.*

aye. The designation for "yes" in voting.

ballot. A sheet of paper used to cast a secret vote.

board of directors. A group of people having advisory or managerial powers who are selected to govern an organization.

business. The matters brought before an *assembly.*

bylaws. A document providing the rules for governing adopted by an organization. See Chapter 2.

call of a meeting. A *notice of meeting* sent to all members announcing the date, time, place, and purpose of a *meeting.*

call to order. Instructions to a member to cease disorderly behavior or a violation of the rules (see Chapter 5); the statement of the *chair* that opens a *meeting.*

called meeting. A *special meeting.*

chair. The person who presides at a *meeting.* See Chapter 3.

close debate. To end discussion of a *motion,* which brings the matter to a vote.

committee. A body of persons elected or appointed to handle a designated task for an *assembly.* See Chapter 3.

committee of the whole. The entire *assembly* while functioning as a *committee.* See Chapter 3.

conference. A *meeting* to discuss matters of common interest.

constitution. A document that provides the basic principles and laws of an organization. See Chapter 2.

convene. To direct a body of people to assemble.

convention. A meeting of people assembled for a common purpose.

credentials committee. A group of people elected or appointed to verify that *delegates* or members are authorized to vote. See Chapter 2.

debate. The discussion of a *motion* that precedes voting. See Chapter 4.

delegate. A person who represents others at a *meeting*.

dilatory. Tending to cause delay, such as a statement or action intended to obstruct proceedings.

division of the assembly. Retaking a vote by voice or show of hands when a count is uncertain or is questioned.

division of a motion. Dividing a complex or cumbersome *motion* into two or more less complex independent motions. See Chapter 4.

ex officio. By virtue of or because of an office, such as when the vice president serves ex officio as president of the Senate.

executive committee or board. A *committee* consisting of the officers of an organization and, often, the immediate past president.

executive session. Any *meeting* or portion of a meeting during which the proceedings are kept secret. See Chapter 3.

floor. Existing before an assembly; a designation of the right to speak in a *meeting*, as in *obtaining the floor*, or being granted the right to speak. See Chapter 4.

in order. Correct in parliamentary terms.

incidental motion. A *motion* that is prompted by or arises from another motion. See Chapter 5.

main motion. Any motion used to introduce *business* at a *meeting*. See Chapter 5.

majority vote. More than one-half of the votes cast, such as fifty-one of one hundred votes.

meeting. A single body, or *assembly,* of people in one location in which the attendees do not separate except for a short *recess.*

minority report. A report of the *committee* members who oppose the committee's majority position. See Chapter 3.

minutes. The official record of proceedings at a *meeting.* See Chapter 3.

motion. A proposal made before an *assembly* for the members' consideration and action; also called "question." See Chapter 5.

move. To make or state a *motion.*

notice of meeting. The official announcement of the date, time, place, and purpose of a *meeting.*

obtaining the floor. Being recognized by the *chair* to address the *assembly.* See Chapter 4.

on the floor. Currently before an *assembly,* such as a *motion* being discussed by the members.

order of business. See *agenda.*

orders of the day. The program of *business* to be conducted and the order in which it is to be conducted.

out of order. A statement or action that is not correct parliamentary practice.

parliamentarian. An authority concerning parliamentary law and practice.

parliamentary authority. A book of *rules of order* that an organization specifies as its binding authority on matters of parliamentary practice. See Chapter 2.

pending motion. A *motion* that is *on the floor.*

plurality. In voting, a number greater than any other but less than half, such as forty votes for a winning candidate, twenty-five for a second candidate, and thirty-five for a third candidate.

point of information. A request for more information.

point of order. A statement that, or a question whether, a matter is *in order.*

point of privilege. A point raised by a member concerning something that adversely affects the members.

precedence. Rank or order of importance, as in the precedence of *motions.* See Chapter 5.

presiding officer. The one who conducts a *meeting.* See Chapter 3.

previous question. A motion that brings debate to a close and puts the motion being considered to an immediate vote.

privileged motion. The highest ranking *motion;* one that is not directly related to any other motion being considered but takes precedence over it and all other motions. See Chapter 5.

proxy. Authority or power to act for someone else as in absentee voting; not recommended for deliberative *assemblies.*

put the question, or motion, to a vote. The statement of the *chair* calling for a vote on a *motion.* See Chapter 4.

question. Another word for *motion.*

quorum. The number of people who must be present at a *meeting* to conduct *business* legally.

receiving a report. Permitting a report to be read to an *assembly.* See Chapter 3.

recess. A less formal break than an adjournment, after which *business* continues where it left off without formally opening the proceedings.

regular meeting. A routine *meeting* scheduled periodically to transact ordinary *business.*

resolution. A formal expression of opinion or purpose that begins with the words "RESOLVED, That _____."

roll-call vote. A voice vote in which members respond yes or no as their names are called.

rules of order. The rules of an organization that pertain to parliamentary procedure in a *meeting.* See Chapter 2.

second. The endorsement of a *motion* by a second member ("I second the motion").

select committee. See *special committee.*

session. A series of *meetings* during which the *business* being transacted or the program being presented is continued from one meeting to another.

sine die. Without day; without a specified day being assigned for a future *meeting.*

special committee. A *committee* elected or appointed to handle a special assignment, after which it is dissolved; also called select committee. See Chapter 3.

special meeting. A *called meeting* held for a special purpose at a time not specified in the *bylaws;* no other action may be taken at a special meeting.

special order. A provision that is adopted to designate a specific time to consider a particular subject rather than bring it up at its scheduled time on the program. See Chapter 5.

standing committee. A permanent *committee* usually provided for in the *bylaws,* as opposed to a temporary *special committee;* a committee appointed for a designated period, such as a year, or for a specific session. See Chapter 3.

standing rules. Rules, in addition to those in the *constitution, bylaws,* and *rules of order,* adopted like ordinary resolutions that continue until rescinded or modified by a majority vote at any *meeting.* See Chapter 2.

subsidiary motion. A *motion* applied to another motion currently being considered as a means of disposing of the other motion; also called a secondary motion. See Chapter 5.

table. To set a *motion* or other matter aside for later consideration.

teleconference. A *meeting* held by electronic linkage, rather than face to face. See *audioconference* and *videoconference.*

teller. Someone appointed or elected to distribute, collect, and count ballots.

unfinished business. Matters carried over from a previous *meeting.*

videoconference. An electronic *meeting* in which the participants are connected by sound and pictures (television). See also *audioconference.*

waiver of notice. A written statement that an organization is not required to notify the signers of a future *meeting* or meetings.

Index